Take Heart

Prayers for the Terminally Ill

Judy Sliger

Take Heart
Prayers for the Terminally Ill

Published by Next Step Books, P.O. Box 70271, West Valley City, Utah 84170

Cover design by Next Step Books, LLC.

ISBN-13: 978-1-937671-14-3
ISBN-10: 1937671143

Dedicated to my family and the many faithful prayer warriors who have carried me throughout this journey.

With deepest appreciation to Pastor Kevin and the staff and members of Northside Baptist Church, Dr. Lynn Parker and the staff at University Women's HealthCare, University OB/GYN Associates, Shelley Roby, ARNP, and the staff at Nova Family Medicine, the staff at Brown Cancer Chemo Center, the staff and volunteers at Brown Cancer Resource Center, Rosella C. Rudd, the staff at Hardin Memorial Hospital Cancer Center and Hardin Memorial Health Information Systems Department, Ms. Misty White and Ms. Jackie Liddington.

Table of Contents

Introduction

One day you or a loved one received the news that an illness had entered the terminal stages. This news started reactions and adjustments you probably thought you'd already worked through. If you're a Christian, you may have felt guilty about the thoughts and emotions that followed. I certainly did.

Since July 2007, I've battled ovarian cancer. The Holy Spirit has used prayer, Bible study, and conversations with others to show me God understands every thought, emotion, and physical sensation we experience. He accepts us and loves us. This book is an attempt to express what I've learned and how God has comforted me through prayer and His people.

If you have loved ones facing death, perhaps you'd like to give them this book for their own use. Or maybe you prefer to pray specific prayers for, or with, them.

If you are currently facing death or major health decisions, you can select a prayer that seems to match your current situation. If you are feeling alone, picture me sitting beside you, holding your hand and praying with you.

After every prayer I've included Scripture passages that have brought me comfort. I encourage you to look them up in the Bible and read the surrounding verses to see various situations the faithful—and not-so-faithful—people of God encountered. Go ahead. Breathe a sigh of relief that you are not a horrible person because of your emotions.

And you can feel the arms of God surround you, too.

"I have told you these things, so that in me you may have peace. In this world you will have trouble. But take heart! I have overcome the world." (John 16:33)

Salvation

God,

I don't understand much theology, but I know I can't go on as things are.

I choose to believe what You said in the Bible—that Jesus is Your only Son who was born fully God, yet fully man, and lived on earth. I understand that only the payment of a perfect life can pay for all the wrongs I've done and thought. Jesus is the only one who has lived that perfect life. I believe He made that payment for me with His death on the Cross and His resurrection three days later.

I'm a sinner. I accept Jesus' gift of salvation. Thank you for sending Your Holy Spirit to live in me and guide and comfort me. Thank you for the gift of eternal life.

Thank you for saving me.

Amen.

For all have sinned and fall short of the glory of God. (Romans 3:23)

But God demonstrates his own love for us in this: While we were still sinners, Christ died for us. (Romans 5:8)

For the wages of sin is death, but the gift of God is eternal life in Christ Jesus our Lord. (Romans 6:23)

That if you declare with your mouth, "Jesus is Lord," and believe in your heart that God raised him from the dead, you will be saved. (Romans 10:9)

Surrender

Lord,

I surrender to You and Your will. I don't understand why You've allowed this pain, deterioration of my body and isolation from others. I haven't really worried about it. My focus has been on how to defeat this illness, then how to live with it, and now how to die from it.

You have shown me that control is an illusion. I cannot control the progression of this illness, my medical team's decisions, the side effects from various treatments, the choice of family and friends to remain involved, or Your will for my life. I've fought this lack of control. I've tried eight types of chemotherapy, exercise, various standard and naturopathic medications, drastic dietary changes, and faith healing. Yet here I am facing death.

I only can determine my response to whatever happens, and I fear I may lose the ability to control that.

So, Lord, once again, I give it all to You. I surrender all my past efforts, all my present circumstances, and all my future. I know I will encounter new fears, possibly have additional pain, and will continue to face physical and emotional changes in the days to come. But nothing is stronger than You and Your love.

I choose to believe You. I surrender all.

Amen.

For I am convinced that neither death nor life, neither angels nor demons, neither the present nor the future, nor any powers, neither height nor depth, nor anything else in all creation, will be able to separate us from the love of God that is in Christ Jesus our Lord. (Romans 8:38-39)

Assurance

Lord,

I need Your assurance I've made the right decision, and it's time to acknowledge that death is coming soon. I accept at this point hospice care is the best option for my loved ones and me. I understand this acceptance is not a lack of faith in Your promises or Your power to heal me.

I know my time is in Your hands and acknowledge that only You have power over life and death. I believe that Your plans for me are for good, never evil; that when I step from this world into Your presence, I will be home, and home will be far more wonderful than I ever dreamed or imagined.

Thank You for being with me every second. Thank You for understanding my doubts and for not being angry with me when they surface.

Thank You for Your assurance and peace in this decision.

Amen.

If any of you lacks wisdom, you should ask God, who gives generously to all without finding fault, and it will be given to you. (James 1:5)

Do not be anxious about anything, but in every situation by prayer and petition with thanksgiving, present your requests to God. And the peace of God which transcends all understanding, will guard your hearts and your minds in Christ Jesus. (Philippians 4:6-7)

Things Undone

Lord,

I pray for things left undone—visits I meant to make to loved ones, letters I meant to write, words I meant to say, and provision for others I didn't consider. I pray You will provide the life lessons I didn't teach my children and advice I didn't give.

I think of all I'll miss with loved ones— sunrises and storms, shared meals and meetings with friends, college graduations, marriages and babies yet unborn snuggled in my arms. I surrender all these to you.

I grieve for experiences I will not have—the smiles of grandchildren, caring for loved ones during their illnesses, and the comfort I will not be able to give in their future sorrows.

I feel selfish, Lord, but I pray for Your consolation for my dreams which will not see reality—trips I won't take, skills I won't master, even movies I won't see.

You hold my dreams, Lord. All times are in Your hand. Help me remember that in Heaven there will be no sorrow, and that I'll find all my fulfillment in You.

Amen.

Being confident of this, that he [God] who began a good work in you will carry it on to completion until the day of Christ Jesus. (Philippians 1:6)

Whatever is has already been, and what will be has been before; and God will call the past to account. (Ecclesiastes 3:15)

My Family

Lord,

I pray for my family. Assure them that the decisions I've made are right for all of us. We each have fears, Father. Help us see that fear is a natural reaction, but we should not remain afraid. Give my family physical, mental, and emotional stamina to face the hours and details of caring for me. Comfort them as they grieve the changes in all our lives. Send friends to encourage them. Provide peace in all the turmoil. Remind them to share their troubles with each other and to bring all their burdens and worries to You.

Protect my loved ones through the ugliness. In the sadness and distastefulness of caring for my failing body, let them rest in the comfort they bring me. When they hear my moans of pain, let them hear the sighs of relief the medication brings. If they see my tears of sadness, let them see my joy in their presence and their care.

Give us happy memories of this time—laughter over the mishaps that will occur, tenderness as we share episodes from our past, and a deepening love for each other and You. Bless us as we carry each other and You carry us all. Remind us that we may be separated temporarily by death, but You have overcome death, and we'll be reunited in Heaven.

Amen.

Carry each other's burdens, and in this way you will fulfill the law of Christ. (Galatians 6:2)

Fear

Lord,

I'm afraid. I'm afraid of pain, possible embarrassment, that I'll lose control of my bodily functions and my mind, that I won't have the help I'll need in this stage of life, that others will hurt me, and that I'll hurt others.

I'm afraid of the unknown. I'm afraid that my belief in you is misplaced. I'm ashamed to admit it, Lord, and I know better, but fear and doubts creep in.

I'm afraid You'll be ashamed of the way I handle dying, that my actions will not honor You.

Help me be aware of Your Presence and Your promises.

Help me refuse to condemn myself or remain trapped in fear.

Thank You for understanding all my fears and doubts and weaknesses. Thank You for loving me through them. Thank you for loving me and carrying me—always.

Amen.

There is no fear in love. But perfect love drives out fear, because fear has to do with punishment. (1John 4:18a)

"I do believe, help me overcome my unbelief!" (Mark 9:24b)

For God hath not given us the spirit of fear; but of power, and of love, and of a sound mind. (2 Timothy 1:7, KJV)

Caregivers

Lord,

Today I pray for all my caregivers—the hospice staff, my family and friends, and everyone else who will work with me in any way.

I pray for their physical health. Protect them from illness and pain. Shield them from infections and viruses. Give them rest and strength.

I pray for their minds. Keep them alert and aware of my physical, mental, emotional and spiritual needs. Show them when and how to meet my needs and the needs of each other.

I pray for their hearts. Lord, how great the temptation must be to seal themselves off from the pain and unpleasantness they encounter when caring for those of us who are dying. They must be tempted to cope by

22

blocking all emotions toward us. I do not want to cause them grief and pain, but I need to know they see me as an individual.

So, Father, keep them tender and caring by transforming harsh realities into kindness and compassion. Turn any dark and painful thoughts into a focus on the comfort and relief they bring me. Protect them from dread. Let them anticipate a smile of welcome and thankfulness from me. And, Lord, make me the patient who always shows gratitude.

Holy God, meet all their needs. Give them safe passage as they travel. Give them restoring sleep. Help them refuse to dwell on worries. Give them Your peace.

Amen.

Then the righteous will answer, 'Lord, when did we see you hungry and feed you, or thirsty and give you something to drink? When did we see you a stranger and invite you in, or needing clothes and clothe you? When did we see you sick or in prison and go to visit you?' The King will reply, 'Truly I tell you, whatever you did for one of the least of these brothers and sisters of mine, you did for me.' (Matthew 25:37-40)

Priorities

Lord,

Set my priorities as I live my final days here. Instead of dwelling only in the past, which is giving up and ignoring the daily blessings You still have for me, let me live in the present. Remind me not to try desperately to plan everyone's future, which is attempting to exert control over circumstances I should give to You.

If there are plans I need to make, bring them to mind and provide the resources I need. If there are people with whom I should speak, provide easy access to them. If there are possessions to be given away, remind me of each item, show me who should have it, and go before me to prevent resentment and greed among the recipients.

Most of all, Lord, prepare my heart. Let me say what You want me to say to each person I encounter. Help me recall ancient wounds to which I contributed, and bring me together with each person I need to forgive or who needs to forgive me. Then pour the balm of Your presence into each encounter, and heal our hearts and souls.

Father, keep me from frantically trying to relive my life or cram what I think I'll be missing into these days. Remind me to be grateful for every moment and to trust each moment to you.

Amen.

There is a time for everything, and a season for every activity under the heavens: (Ecclesiastes 3:1)

Organization

Lord,

Help my family and me with organization. The many details we must handle overwhelm us.

Help us keep track of whom to call for different needs and questions. Direct us to the person at each place who will remember me and my unique needs, so we don't continually have to explain that this pain medication nauseates me, an inactive ingredient in this generic drug gives me a migraine, or this adult diaper causes a rash.

Help us set up a system, so we can keep track of appointments, the times various health care professionals will be here, when to order prescription refills, which medications to take at which times, and which medications have precautions and conditions for administration. Prevent delays with deliveries and appointments, and help everyone arrive at the proper time.

Help us to organize all the sitters who come to help us. Show us how to communicate with everyone involved with my care about operating machinery, cleaning me, properly preparing my food, where and how to record medications and procedures performed, and the location of all information and supplies. Help us reorganize our home to make everything accessible to helpers while maintaining a welcoming, comfortable atmosphere.

Finally, Lord, organize my thoughts and energy to honor You, and to focus on Your priorities and promises instead of my temporary afflictions.

Amen.

In their hearts, humans plan their course, but the LORD establishes their steps. (Proverbs 16:9)

Relief from Pain

Lord,

I'm afraid of pain. I'm afraid I will embarrass myself when I hurt. I'm afraid my doctors won't realize how much pain I'm in and won't prescribe adequate medication. I'm afraid there isn't adequate medication, or that it will increase my nausea after it's administered. I'm afraid that my caregivers won't realize that addiction isn't an issue and that they won't give me my pain medication when I need it. I'm afraid someone coming into my home will steal my pain meds. I'm afraid I'll inadvertently be a stumbling block to a curious youth or a friend recovering from drug abuse, that they'll take a dose of my narcotic and spiral into addiction.

I'm afraid pain will rob me of these limited days I have with my loved ones; that it will keep me from doing what I want to do, from fulfilling my purpose for still being here. I'm afraid pain will reduce me to sleeping away too much of this precious time.

Help me trust You through every minute and every fear.

Amen.

"Which of you, if your son asks for bread, will give him a stone? Or if he asks for a fish, will give him a snake? If you, then, though you are evil, know how to give good gifts to your children, how much more will your Father in heaven give good gifts to those who ask him!" (Matthew 7:9-11)

Respect and Consideration

Lord,

Today I pray for respect—respect for me and from me. Please remind those who come in contact with me that I am a unique person, not chart 1127414, not that woman with cancer, not that incontinent patient with bedsores. Help my caregivers speak gently and, as much as possible, respect my privacy. Help them find ways to preserve my dignity as they administer medication, bathe or move my deteriorating body, and change my bandages, diapers or bedding. Help them remember that I hear their comments when I'm in a light doze, that the light they turned on may be glaring directly in my eyes, that the music they're playing may intensify my headache, and that perfume or microwaved meals may increase my nausea.

Lord, remind me to respect others. Help me make requests, not demands. Remind me to thank those who visit and care for me each time they are here. If time permits, Father, show me how I can minister to each person I encounter.

Thank You for each person You bring into my life. Help us all to remember that before the world was formed, You planned for each of us to be, that each of us is the apple of Your eye.

Amen.

So in everything, do to others what you would have them to do to you, for this sums up the Law and the Prophets. (Matthew 7:12)

Show proper respect to everyone.... (1 Peter 2:17a)

Awareness

Lord,

I pray for awareness of Your presence, Your guidance and Your comfort. Help me be aware of the moments. Don't let me think of them as the incessant drip of a leaky faucet, counting away my life. Make me aware of the beauty in each moment—the smiles of a loved one, a beam of sunshine, the comfort of a clean, soft pillowcase, or the lawn care worker singing outside my window.

Make me aware of others. Remind me of their love and concern for me. Let me thank them for their involvement, and let me bring happiness, comfort or laughter into our visits. Show me how to talk with them about their grief or pain in seeing me suffer. Help us discuss their worries about our future separation. Show me other needs they have which I can meet. Then give me the awareness, desire and resources to help them.

Make me aware of my limitations and false pride. Remind me that pushing too hard will result not only in extra pain for me but in extra work for my caregivers if I take on responsibilities You never meant me to have. Help me recognize when I need help. Then give me the grace to ask for that assistance.

When I need rest, help me be gracious in letting others know. Help me state my needs in a way that lets others be glad that they can provide respite rather than resenting my cutting a conversation or a visit short.

Most of all, Lord, make me aware of You—Your continuous presence, Your guidance and Your comfort. Let my moments here make others aware of You and draw them to You.

Amen.

The LORD is near to all who call on him, to all who call on him in truth. (Psalm 145:18)

Praise be to the God and Father of our Lord Jesus Christ, the Father of compassion and the God of all comfort, who comforts us in all our troubles, so that we can comfort those in any trouble with the comfort we ourselves have received from God. (2 Corinthians 1:3-4)

Those Who Think I Should Keep Fighting

Lord,

I pray for those who think I should keep fighting, for those who think I am choosing to die.

I understand that my decision seems contradictory to Your promises for healing. Sometimes healing in heaven seems like rationalizing. Maybe I'm making excuses for my lack of faith in Your promises, or I'm hiding from examining myself for unconfessed sin, or even dancing around whether You are, indeed, love.

But, Father, You have given me peace about this decision and its ramifications. I know that I am in Your will and that You are with me.

So, I pray for all of us—for me to have unwavering faith, for others to accept that

You have chosen a different path for me than what they and I preferred, and that I would have patience with them.

Open their hearts and minds to accept my circumstances. Help them see that neither I, nor they, control the number of my days. Give us assurance that You are with them and me every step of the way. Help us hold fast to the knowledge that Your ways are not our ways, that Your thoughts are so far above our thoughts that we can't begin to fathom Your purposes and Your love.

Help us trust that Your plans, especially in my dying, are only to bring me good.

Amen.

For my thoughts are not your thoughts, neither are your ways my ways," declares the LORD. (Isaiah 55:8)

However, as it is written: "What no eye has seen, what no ear has heard, and what no human mind has conceived"—the things God has prepared for those who love him—these are the things God has revealed to us by his Spirit. (I Corinthians 2:9)

Giving Up

Lord,

Forgive me for all the times I give up. I don't mean submitting to Your will and Your work in my life. I mean all the times I quit trying.

I've given up on others. "Joan doesn't care about me. If she did, she'd at least call me." I've given up on my church. "These people sending me cards don't even know me. Why don't they at least call me or visit me?" I've given up on my family. "Don't they know I'm sick? Why can't Jenny go through the drive-through and bring home dinner? Why can't Stan run the washer? Why can't Bob buy the groceries?"

I've given up on You. Instead of praying about a decision, I say, "God has placed me in a time of medical science and directed me to wise doctors. I need to do whatever they say." I've given up on the idea of healing. "My immune system has broken down. God can do anything; earthly healing must not be part of His plan for me." I've given up on Your basic nature, Your total love for me. "God created me with a genetic defect. I'm just a dispensable part. He doesn't think I'm important enough to remain on earth."

I've given up on bringing all these lies to You, so I can see them for what they are, attempts by Satan to hurt both You and me by keeping me from coming to You about everything and experiencing your healing. Satan cannot defeat You, so he wants to hurt You. Any parent knows when someone hurts a child, he hurts the parent, and You are my Father.

And, Father, thank You for never giving up on me.

Amen.

The LORD will vindicate me; your love, LORD, endures forever—do not abandon the works of your hands. (Psalm 138:8)

Anger

Lord,

Help me with my anger. You have said, "Be angry and sin not," so I know anger itself is not a sin. Help me acknowledge my anger. Help me realize why I'm angry and with whom or what I'm angry.

Channel my anger in healthy ways. I can no longer take a walk, hammer nails, knead dough or clean house to work off this excess emotion. Please keep me from fussing at my family or sniping at my caregivers or grumbling to my nurses. Help me remember all these people have their own stressors, and that I don't want to add to their load.

Lord, heal my unwholesome anger. Help me recognize it immediately. Show me how to dig it up and destroy it instead of nurturing it into bitterness. Give me insight into misunderstandings. If someone offers well-meant but inappropriate comments, give me a gracious way to stop that thread of conversation. Help me redirect our time into pleasant activities. After they're gone, help me give that situation to you instead of nursing a grudge.

Lord, show me how to use my anger. Are there organizations that could help me with an unmet healthcare need? Are there groups who could use my story to help others? Guide me to them, and help me provide the information they need about my situation to ease the way for me or for others.

Thank you for giving me anger. Help me handle it in ways that honor you.

Amen.

"In your anger do not sin": Do not let the sun go down while you are still angry, and do not give the devil a foothold.... Do not let any unwholesome talk come out of your mouths, but only what is helpful for building others up according to their needs, that it may benefit those who listen. (Ephesians 4:26-27, 29)

What Might Have Been

Lord,

Protect me from dwelling on what might have been. Help me focus on what is.

I look at my husband and picture the trips we planned to take, the restaurants where we meant to eat, the friends we promised to visit, and the projects we were going to tackle. I look at my child. I'll miss his college graduation, his career, meeting the love of his life, his marriage, and the birth of his children.

I imagine how I would have spent a normal lifespan, the articles and books I wanted to write, the flowerbeds I wanted to plant, the quilts I wanted to piece, the friendships I wanted to savor, and the memories I wanted to make with my family. And grief overwhelms me at what will not be.

You've shown me that I have a choice, Lord. I can dwell on what might have been, and my grief will turn to anger, my anger to

40

despair, and my despair to withdrawal. All will isolate me from enjoying what I have now, will dishearten those I love, and will keep all of us from enjoying the time You have given us.

As my body relentlessly deteriorates, You continually provide me with joy and comfort—helping a friend select her mother-of-the-groom dress, phone calls from a high school friend, an entire meal without nausea, the purple petunias blooming on the deck, and bouquets from visitors (without my usual runny nose).

You have shown me there is a time to mourn, but there is also a time to dance. Help me dance to the beat of the days You have given me.

Amen.

There is a time for everything, and a season for every activity under the heavens: a time to be born and a time to die, a time to plant and a time to uproot, a time to kill and a time to heal, a time to tear down and a time to build, a time to weep and a time to laugh, a time to mourn and a time to dance.... (Ecclesiastes 3:1-4)

Healing for My Loved Ones

Lord,

Please provide healing for my loved ones. You know better than anyone how they feel. You know how suppressed emotions can smolder and bring illness, misunderstanding and separation.

Help them recognize and understand that their emotions are not sin and are natural— grief at the realization that my death is imminent; anger that neither they, the doctors, nor I can physically heal me; frustration that all our lives have irrevocably changed; resentment that they must suffer losses years earlier than most people; betrayal that You, the Creator and Master of everything, could have healed me on Earth, and You did not; isolation from others because of the demands of my poor health, isolation from others who haven't gone through this experience, isolation when they sink into their emotions instead of bringing them to You. And guilt—oh, God, the guilt—that we even feel these emotions, that we think any hint of an unpleasant feeling is sin, and that sometimes we simply don't trust You enough.

God, I can't begin to comprehend all Your whys and all Your ways. But I know that You, too, have emotions, that Your heart hurts for us as we suffer through all these feelings. I know healing and comfort are in Your hands for all of us. Help my loved ones understand that while we may never understand Your ways, we can always know that Your love, Your patience and Your presence carry us.

Amen.

"I have told you these things, so that in me you may have peace. In this world you will have trouble. But take heart! I have overcome the world." (John 16:33)

Releasing Wasted Time

Lord,

I pray for time I feel I have wasted. You know the toll this illness has taken on me— the overwhelming fatigue, the nausea, the bone-deep pain and muscle aches, and the mental fog. I feel I'm moving toward an ill-defined destination without anticipation or purpose. I sleep, I play computer games, I read, sometimes I even pray, but I don't spend my time productively.

I look at others in my situation. They flit around the country visiting friends. They give speeches to medical students and organize fundraisers for noble causes while I have to double count the change before I pay at the drive-through window. I'm envious of their energy and focus and condemn myself for my laziness and lack of initiative.

But You comfort me in my confinement. You help me sift through my emotions and my reactions. You encourage me with a friend's brief phone call. You use light fiction to remind me You are always present. You show me festering thoughts that isolate me from others and put a barrier between You and me, and then heal me of that infected thinking.

You show me how precious and powerful prayer is.

So, Lord, help me remember that time spent healing is not wasted. Help me realize that reading, a phone conversation, even a game or two of Solitaire, are healthy alternatives to dwelling on my illness. Remind me that when I surrender my moments to You, You will teach me to number my days.

Amen.

Teach us to number our days, that we may gain a heart of wisdom. (Psalm 90:12)

Therefore we do not lose heart. Though outwardly we are wasting away, yet inwardly we are being renewed day by day. For our light and momentary troubles are achieving for us an eternal glory that far outweighs them all. So we fix our eyes not on what is seen, but on what is unseen, since what is seen is temporary, but what is unseen is eternal. (2 Corinthians 4:16-17)

The Lost

Lord,

I pray for those who do not know you as their Savior, especially those in my family. My heart breaks at the thought that the last time I will see them is the last moment I am conscious of their presence here on Earth.

I know that You draw everyone to You. I know that You are not willing that any should perish. I know that You cry out for all those You want to save who reject You. I know that You stand at the door and knock. I know that You love my family more than I ever could.

I know that You will work all things for good, so Father, please let my death draw them to You. Let the peace You give me shine through any pain, sorrow, anger, or doubts I might show. In the middle of this prolonged parting, Lord, let them see that the way through the loneliness and loss that follow the death of a loved one is You.

Father, save them. Somehow, break through that barrier that separates them from You. Help them realize they can never earn Your love, they can never be better than your love, and they can never be complete without Your love.

Oh, God, my deepest desire is for them to accept Your gift of salvation. I don't know what else to say, Lord, except that when I am beyond words, Your Spirit groans with utterances too deep to mention. Groan for them, Sweet Spirit, groan for them.

Amen.

In the same way, the Spirit helps us in our weakness. We do not know what we ought to pray for, but the Spirit himself intercedes for us through wordless groans. (Romans 8:26)

The Lord is not slow in keeping his promise, as some understand slowness. Instead he is patient with you, not wanting anyone to perish, but everyone to come to repentance. (2 Peter 3:9)

Expectations

Lord,

I can't live up to expectations. I know You've gotten me to this point, but my friends and family pile on expectations I cannot meet. I keep telling them I am weak and whiny; they keep telling me I'm brave.

Father, I thank You that they don't turn from me in disgust. But I'm crumbling under the weight of their expectations. You know that I moan, I complain, I whine, I sob, I pout—no, I pitch full-fledged temper tantrums. I project a false front. I disguise my frustrations with ineffective medications and treatments as prayer requests. Instead of admitting my impatience, I request prayer for all the overworked professionals who help me. Rather than confess my resentment that You haven't already miraculously, instantly healed me, I tell others the latest medical update.

And I'm doing it again, Lord, but this time with You.

Lord, I want to be healed. I don't want to have another smidgen of pain, nausea, joint or muscle aches, sinus pressure, nosebleeds, itchy skin, flashing lights, floaters, or depression. I want to see my son graduate from college and marry a wonderful young woman. I want to cuddle their babies. I want to grow old gracefully and with heretofore-unseen beauty with my husband. Curly hair would be nice, too.

I want total transparency with everyone I love. Then I want them to love me just as much without being disappointed in me and without expecting me to be a super saint.

But You are Lord. Your promises are true. You have not cursed me with this illness, this dying. Rather, You carry me. You make a way for me. You weep for me. You intercede for me.

So, Lord, I thank you that Your expectation is simply that I cling to you, and that when I don't, You still cling to me. You will never let me go.

Amen.

But he said to me, "My grace is sufficient for you, for my power is made perfect in weakness." Therefore, I will boast all the more gladly about my weaknesses, so that Christ's power may rest on me. That is why, for Christ's sake, I delight in weaknesses, in insults, in hardships, in persecutions, in difficulties. For when I am weak, then I am strong. (2 Corinthians 12:9-10)

Healing of Memories

Lord,

I pray You'll heal my memories. For years, I have harbored resentment that You did not spare my father and my sister from lengthy deaths, that they lingered—Daddy paralyzed and Nancy on a J-peg tube for hydration as she medically starved to death. They loved You and served You faithfully, and I thought You should have shown them more mercy.

I lie here tonight remembering the details of their deaths. I never saw my sister mourn being confined to a very few ounces of liquids to remain hydrated, hearing she should no longer leave her bed, and realizing that her keen teacher's mind was fading. I fear that I will not have her strength to witness for You. I remember my father looking into the distance, enduring pain and increasing paralysis. I never heard him complain through those five months. I don't have his quiet courage, my sister's brave acceptance.

I'm crying and griping about a little nausea, and I can still walk and prepare my medicine, choose and digest my food, and ask my loved ones for comfort.

And I realize that You shielded them. Daddy didn't know that many lung cancer patients suffocate, and he died in his sleep from pneumonia. Nancy didn't know that she would survive nine weeks instead of a few days. You provided her with compassionate hospice workers, committed to sparing her pain. You surrounded both of them with people who supported and helped care for them. They died in the midst of love.

And You will provide for all my needs.

Thank you for healing my memories.

Amen.

So I reflected on all this and concluded that the righteous and the wise and what they do are in God's hands....(Ecclesiastes 9:1a)

Innocence

Lord,

I pray for restored innocence. I have always wanted to know why, how much, and when. Particularly through this illness I have insisted on knowledge. I've researched, questioned, and asked others further on this journey about their experiences. Like Eve, I've demanded the knowledge of good and evil when You would have spared me an awareness of things that may not happen.

Consequently, throughout this illness, I've battled fear. I've chided myself with, "Cowards die 1,000 times before their death. The valiant never taste of death but once." Isn't that yet another proof of Your love? Those lines are from Shakespeare's play. But Your word says You will never leave me or forsake me, that You are with me and comfort me in the valley of the shadow of death. You comfort, not condemn.

Lord, forgive me for seeking to know all. I sought too much knowledge for myself, and I'm through with that.

Thank You, Lord, that You show me how Satan is trying to tempt me into unnecessary research so I will fear, but that You always provide a way out of every temptation. Thank You, Lord, that I do not truly know the form my death will take. Thank You for Your constant presence. Help me turn to You rather than dwelling on possibilities.

Amen

No temptation has overtaken you except what is common to mankind. And God is faithful; he will not let you be tempted beyond what you can bear. But when you are tempted, he will also provide a way out so that you can endure it. (1 Corinthians 10:13)

Wakefulness in the Middle of the Night

Lord,

Here I am again, the only one awake in the middle of the night. You know how Satan assaults me at these times. Nightmares haunt me. Regrets for past sins, ones I know You've forgiven, try to entrap me. Old hurts try to regain a foothold. Pain grapples with me. Fear tries to overpower me.

Although my family is in the same house, I feel isolated. Friends would welcome the chance to encourage me during a 2 a.m. phone call, but I don't want to press those numbers.

But You are the Lord of all. You separated the evening and the morning and declared them both good. You created beauty in the dark. You are with me in the watches of the night.

Over the years you have taught me I can flounder in fear or I can reflect on You.

So tonight, Lord, I choose to reflect on Your word. Thank You, Father, for speaking to me.

Amen.

He will cover you with his feathers, and under his wings you will find refuge; his faithfulness will be your shield and rampart. You will not fear the terror of night, nor the arrow that flies by day, nor the pestilence that stalks in the darkness, nor the plague that destroys at midday. A thousand may fall at your side, ten thousand at your right hand, but it will not come near you. (Psalm 91:4-7)

In peace, I will lie down and sleep, for you alone, LORD, make me dwell in safety. (Psalm 4:8)

On my bed I remember you; I think of you through the watches of the night. Because you are my help, I sing in the shadow of your wings. I cling to you; your right hand upholds me. (Psalm 63:6-7)

Uselessness

Lord,

I feel useless. I believe You have a plan for each of us and that I'm not following mine. I'm impatient that You haven't shone a spotlight on my path and You haven't directed me to noble tasks. I don't have the energy to serve on a committee. My weakened immune system keeps me from regular church attendance. I don't have the technical knowledge to act on my idea for an online Sunday School class. I can't even cook a meal for a sick friend because the odors nauseate me.

Father, I thank You that I am not useless to You. Before I was born, You planned for my existence. Help me see the opportunities You've given me in this isolation. In my mentally alert moments, I can write encouraging notes. I can call friends in physical or emotional pain.

And always, Lord, I can pray. You've repeatedly shown me the power of prayer. So, Lord, when I feel useless, help me recognize immediately that this is Satan's attempt to distract me from prayer. Direct my thoughts to the person, event, or topic needing Your intervention.

If there is another task for me to accomplish, direct me to it. Protect me from any physical or mental side effects that would interfere. Show me how to manage my medications, my diet and my energy.

Thank You that I always have a purpose in You.

Amen.

For we are God's handiwork, created in Christ Jesus to do good works, which God prepared in advance for us to do. (Ephesians 2:10)

And pray in the Spirit on all occasions with all kinds of prayers and requests. With this in mind, be alert and always keep on praying for all the Lord's people. (Ephesians 6:18)

Well-Intentioned Friends

Lord,

Today I pray for everyone who means well, but offers an insulting or clichéd insight or suggestion. You know the litany, Lord—"God has a purpose for your illness." "All of us are going to die." "No one knows how long he'll live." "God isn't through with you yet." "God has something to teach you." "Each of us should live every day as though it is our last." "Have you examined yourself for the sin that is holding you back?" "Christians die from illness only because they lack faith."

And then there are those who assure me if I'll go to this doctor, or that hospital, or seek this naturopathic treatment, or stop all treatment because my life is in Your hands and any medical intervention is a lack of faith in Your power, that I'll be healed.

I do learn from each of these comments. I learn patience and to be slow to speak. I've realized that sometimes the comment actually is a revelation to the speaker, rather than a commentary on my life. You've repeatedly reminded me that each speaker is attempting to comfort or encourage me in a situation that none of us really understands. But lately, Lord, You've shown me another reason for such well-meaning words of no comfort. They're a glimpse into that person's rationalization. If they can figure out a reason I still face dying after this long struggle with cancer, they can avoid that particular mistake or lack of awareness they hope I have. If they don't make the same mistake, they won't get cancer, and they won't face a similar death.

With this realization, You've flooded me with compassion for that person's unspoken fear. And You've given me enough comfort for us all. You are always with us.

So, thank You, Lord, for the lessons I've learned from well-intentioned friends.

Amen.

And surely I am with you always, to the very end of the age. (Matthew 28:20b)

Endurance

Lord,

Help me endure. Sometimes a little voice whispers, "You don't have to do this. You have enough pain medication to end this peacefully. Why don't you wait until everyone is asleep or out of the house, then take enough pills to end all this misery?"

You know how tempting that voice can be. You, alone, know about all the times the pain medication fails, the nausea rises, and the muscles and bones ache. (Flu-like symptoms? *Hmphh!*)

But more, Lord, You know how negative thoughts attack. They slip in, those memories of loved ones' final illnesses, mental snapshots of their sores and wasted limbs, and flashbacks of their frustration as their confused brains imprisoned the words they wanted to say. My constant nemesis, fear, tries to convince me that the details I'll face as I die are too overwhelming for You to handle, that Your grace will not be sufficient, that I am a burden and a hindrance to others, and that remaining on Earth only to die soon is pointless. Satan tells me I have grieved You and that You'll ultimately take me to heaven, but that I must face death alone. And that is the biggest lie of all—that You are not always with me.

Only You know the course of this race, the narrow lanes, the turns, the hurdles and the final laps. And You have not abandoned me. You have not left me comfortless. You have never—and will not *ever*—leave me.

Thank You, Father, for Your presence, Your comfort and Your encouragement. Help me reject that insidious voice and turn to you.

Amen.

Therefore, since we are surrounded by such a great cloud of witnesses, let us throw off everything that hinders and the sin that so easily entangles. And let us run with perseverance the race marked out for us, fixing our eyes on Jesus, the pioneer and perfecter of faith. (Hebrews 12:1)

When you pass through the waters, I will be with you; and when you pass through the rivers, they will not sweep over you. When you walk through the fire, you will not be burned; the flames will not set you ablaze. For I am the LORD your God, the Holy One of Israel, your Savior. (Isaiah 43:2-3a)

Survivor's Guilt

Lord,

Lately I've been thinking of those I've met who have died prematurely. For longer than I want to admit, I've wanted my struggle to be finished. If healing on Earth isn't Your plan for me, I don't want to be here any longer. Once again, I fear the possible physical pain, the emotional pain of my loved ones, and the secret fears watching me die may instill in them. And I am ashamed.

Every moment You give me here is precious, and I'm complaining because I am still here. I feel so guilty, not only for my ingratitude, but because so many people desperately wanted to live and endured harsh treatments I'd never consider. Yet they died, and I'm alive, and I'm whining about it.

Father, I don't understand why You keep me here while others who fought so hard to live—and did so well at it—are home with You. I look at the ones who were mothers with young children, the writers who communicated so beautifully, and the people who shared their joy, their courage, and their zest for life. They died, and I'm here, questioning and complaining and afraid of every future step.

And I remember, Lord, when Peter asked You about Your plans for John. Every version of the Bible I've read states it eloquently, but essentially You told Peter to mind his own business and let You run the world.

So, Lord, once again You've made me smile when I realize You answered my questions centuries ago. And I can sense You're smiling, too.

Thank You for your patience with me. Thank You that Your plan for each of Your children is for our good. Thank You for helping me realize that dealing with my life is enough for me to handle. I don't have to worry about Your plan for others.

Amen.

Peter turned and saw that the disciple whom Jesus loved was following them....When Peter saw him, he asked, "Lord, what about him?" Jesus answered, "If I want him to remain alive until I return, what is that to you? You must follow me." (John 21:20-22)

Cleansing of My Home

Lord,

So much has happened in my home as I wait to join You. We have laughed, shared, wept, cared, rejoiced and forgiven. But we have also experienced turmoil, the physical side effects of my illness, anger, unanswered questions, ugliness, and, soon, my death.

So, Lord, I pray for cleansing of my home after I die. I pray for physical cleansing—that the memories from the odors of the illness, the sounds of machinery, sorrow, pain, and nausea will vanish. I pray that when my family and friends see my empty bed or chair that You will remind them of smiles and laughter, hugs and handclasps. When they step into the kitchen and I no longer stand at the sink, heal their loneliness.

I pray that sorrow at my absence will give way to joy for my release, appreciation of the experiences we shared, and anticipation of our reunion in heaven.

Father, if one of my loved ones has not accepted You as Savior, use my life and death with its happiness and sorrows, advice and mistakes, conversations, laughter and weeping to draw that person to You.

Uproot any bitterness I may have caused, heal any hurts I inflicted, bless and multiply any caring I gave, and let my finite love be magnified into the overpowering love and purpose and plan You have for each of these people You created.

Lord, cleanse my home, my heart, and my loved ones, and bring us all to our real home: You.

Amen.

This is what the LORD says: "I will restore the fortunes of Jacob's tents and have compassion on his dwellings; the city will be rebuilt on her ruins, and the palace will stand in its proper place. From them will come songs of thanksgiving and the sound of rejoicing. (Jeremiah 30:18-19a)

Envy

Lord,

Forgive me for my envy. I envy others for their sense of purpose, their mobility, their freedom, their innocence, and their ignorance.

Father, I even envy other cancer patients. I envy those who have a "good" cancer—one with multiple effective treatment choices, ones where more research has been and is being done, ones whose treatment can be targeted to their specific cancer cells. I envy the ones who have more courage, the ones who persist in life, who say, "I'm going to Europe, anyway." "I'm going to visit my relatives in Des Moines." "I'm blogging weekly." "I'm participating in a clinical study." I envy them when they have the energy and resources to raise awareness and educate others about their cancer.

All I know to do, Lord, is confess my envy, to expose it to Your light and love, and to pray for Your forgiveness.

Thank You, Lord, for showing me this deeply rooted, corrosive sin, and thank You for forgiving me. Thank You for Your love, Your grace, and Your restoration.

Amen

If we confess our sins, he is faithful and will forgive us our sins and purify us from all unrighteousness. (1John 1:9)

Good-byes

Lord,

Today and every day please be with me when I tell a loved one good-bye. At times a simple "Bye. See you soon. Have a safe trip," overwhelms me. As I'm waving good-bye to a departing loved one, grief and fear assail me. I'm not always able to hide the tears. Sometimes I truly am saying a final farewell here on Earth, but most of these are people I expect to see again.

Other times I am overwhelmed by how much I'll miss of their future lives—nephews and nieces in school plays, my child's marriage and children, even the funerals of older loved ones who thought they'd die long before me.

So, Lord, help me during good-byes. Keep the tears back until each person is out of sight. Let their memories be of my smile and love as I wave them on. And, Father, if I fail in this, remind them and me that all of our times are in Your hands. Help us remember that separations are temporary and all of us who know You will see each other again.

Amen.

Trust in him at all times, you people; pour out your hearts to him, for God is our refuge. (Psalm 62:8)

He will be the sure foundation for your times, a rich store of salvation and wisdom and knowledge; the fear of the LORD is the key to this treasure. (Isaiah 33:6)

Those Who Think I Should Have Refused All Medical Treatment

This seems a strange subject to pray about when I am dying. In the past six years, no one has raised the question of why I fought to survive cancer. One night a friend asked me to pray about this—not because she thought I was disobedient to God but to show others how God's will for me was to fight using "traditional" medical treatment. She asked me to explain why I didn't accept the discovery of the tumor, ask for divine intervention, then wait for it—no more doctors, no surgery, no ventures into naturopathy, chemotherapy, countless blood tests, all kinds of medical imagery, or the latest diet that would restore my body to perfect balance and possibly destroy any disease, illness or invader.

I wish I could have taken that route. But the day I received my pelvic ultrasound set me on a different course. I thought I was going to be part of a medical study for early intervention, and my sole contribution would be a periodic mildly uncomfortable pelvic ultrasound.

When the nurse told me I had a "rather large ovarian mass," my sister's prolonged death from ovarian cancer flashed through my mind. A few minutes later I sat in the tennis court parking lot waiting for the end of my 12-year-old son's lesson. I had already called my physician assistant's office for a CA-125 cancer blood test. She had dropped whatever she was doing to come to the phone.

"Take your son straight home. Get him settled. Then come here for your blood draw," she'd instructed.

I held the cell phone and prayed after she disconnected. And God told me through an undeniably clear, strong thought, "Judy, you have cancer, and you're going to have chemo. It will be all right."

He never promised I would be healed. He never told me I would not struggle. He said it would be all right. All right—not okay, not easy, not pain-free, but right.

So stubbornly, often reluctantly, frequently grumbling and weeping and whining, for over six years, I have had surgery and persisted through multiple regimens of chemotherapy. I've tried various diets and naturopathic drugs. I've visited faith healers and had godly people lay hands on me and pray for total healing. I've exercised—well, a little. I've taken enough prescription medication to stock a pharmacy.

So, Lord,

Today I pray for those who believe I never should have begun medical treatment. I still don't like this, Lord. I'm on chemotherapy regimen number seven, number eight if we count Arimidex. I am not healed, and the cancer marker continues to rise. The side effects intensify and grow harder to alleviate.

But You have blessed me through it all. You've surrounded me with caring coworkers, friends and family and dedicated medical staff. You've escorted me through some unpleasant encounters and given me compassionate doctors, nurses and medical assistants. You've smoothed the way innumerable times. You've provided financial, medical and emotional resources in ways I never could have imagined. You continually give me comfort, love, peace, and joy through others and through Your Holy Spirit.

So, I am listening, Lord. I pray for all those who have been on this journey with me, that my experiences will encourage them. I pray for all those who feel I should have followed a different way to deal with cancer, that their frustrations and bitterness should melt away. I pray for all those who will read this book, that the prayers will direct them to You.

I trust You to lead me. I've learned I won't see much of the path ahead, but I trust You to lead me to the end of my earthly journey at Your appointed time. I thank You that You will lead any who come to You.

Amen.

Yea, though I walk through the valley of the shadow of death, I will fear no evil: for thou art with me; thy rod and thy staff they comfort me. Thou preparest a table before me in the presence of mine enemies: thou anointest my head with oil; my cup runneth over. Surely goodness and mercy shall follow me all the days of my life: and I will dwell in the house of the LORD for ever. (Psalm 23:4-6, KJV)

For I know the plans I have for you," declares the LORD, "plans to prosper you and not to harm you, plans to give you hope and a future. (Jeremiah 29:11)

Scripture Passages

Passages are arranged in the order they are found in the Bible. Each passage is followed by the prayer where it is used and the page where it is found. All references are NIV unless otherwise noted.

Old Testament

Psalm 4:8 – In peace, I will lie down and sleep, for you alone, LORD, make me dwell in safety. [Wakefulness in the Middle of the Night, page 54]

Psalm 23:4-6 – Yea, though I walk through the valley of the shadow of death, I will fear no evil: for thou art with me; thy rod and thy staff they comfort me. Thou preparest a table before me in the presence of mine enemies: thou anointest my head with oil; my cup runneth over. Surely goodness and mercy shall follow me all the days of my life: and I will dwell in the house of the LORD forever. [KJV] [Those Who Think I Should Have Refused All Medical Treatment, page 70]

Psalm 62:8 – Trust in him at all times, you people; pour out your hearts to him, for God is our refuge. [Good-byes, page 68]

Psalm 63:6-7 On my bed I remember you; I think of you through the watches of the night. Because you are my help, I sing in the shadow of your wings. I cling to you; your right hand upholds me. [Wakefulness in the Middle of the Night, page 54]

Psalm 90:12 – Teach us to number our days, that we may gain a heart of wisdom. [Releasing Wasted Time, page 44]

Psalm 91:4-7 – He will cover you with his feathers, and under his wings you will find refuge; his faithfulness will be your shield and rampart. You will not fear the terror of night, nor the arrow that flies by day, nor the pestilence that stalks in the darkness, nor the plague that destroys at midday. A thousand may fall at your side, ten thousand at your right hand, but it will not come near you. [Wakefulness in the Middle of the Night, page 54]

Psalm 138:8 – The LORD will vindicate me; your love, LORD, endures forever—do not abandon the works of your hands. [Giving Up, page 36]

Psalm 145:18 – The LORD is near to all who call on him, to all who call on him in truth. [Awareness, page 32]

Proverbs 16:9 – In their hearts, humans plan their course, but the LORD establishes their steps. [Organization, page 26]

Ecclesiastes 3:1 – There is a time for everything, and a season for every activity under the heavens: [Priorities, page 24]

Ecclesiastes 3:1-4 – There is a time for everything, and a season for every activity under the heavens: a time to be born and a time to die, a time to plant and a time to uproot, a time to kill and a time to heal, a time to tear down and a time to build, a time to weep and a time to laugh, a time to mourn and a time to dance, [What Might Have Been, page 40]

Ecclesiastes 3:15 – Whatever is has already been, and what will be has been before; and God will call the past to account. [Things Undone, page 16]

Ecclesiastes 9:1a – So I reflected on all this and concluded that the righteous and the wise and what they do are in God's hands. [Healing of Memories, page 50]

Isaiah 33:6 – He will be the sure foundation for your times, a rich store of salvation and wisdom and knowledge; the fear of the LORD is the key to this treasure. [Good-byes, page 68]

Isaiah 43:2-3a – When you pass through the waters, I will be with you; and when you pass through the rivers, they will not sweep over you. When you walk through the fire, you will not be burned; the flames will not set you ablaze. For I am the LORD your God, the Holy One of Israel, your Savior; [Endurance, page 60]

Isaiah 55:8 – For my thoughts are not your thoughts, neither are your ways my ways," declares the LORD. [Those Who Think I Should Keep Fighting, page 34]

Jeremiah 29:11 – For I know the plans I have for you," declares the LORD, "plans to prosper you and not to harm you, plans to give you hope and a future. [Those Who Think I Should Have Refused All Medical Treatment, page 70]

Jeremiah 30:18-19a – This is what the LORD says: "I will restore the fortunes of Jacob's tents and have compassion on his dwellings; the city will be rebuilt on her ruins, and the palace will stand in its proper place. From them will come songs of thanksgiving and the sound of rejoicing. [Cleansing of My Home, page 64]

New Testament

Matthew 7:9-11 – "Which of you, if your son asks for bread, will give him a stone? Or if he asks for a fish, will give him a snake? If you, then, though you are evil, know how to give good gifts to your children, how much more will your Father in heaven give good gifts to those who ask him! [Relief from Pain, page 28]

Matthew 7:12 – So in everything, do to others what you would have them to do to you, for this sums up the Law and the Prophets. [Respect and Consideration, page 30]

Matthew 25:37-40 – "Then the righteous will answer him, 'Lord, when did we see you hungry and feed you, or thirsty and give you something to drink? When did we see you a stranger and invite you in, or needing clothes and clothe you? When did we see you sick or in prison and go to visit you?' The King will reply, 'Truly I tell you, whatever you did for one of the least of these brothers and sisters of mine, you did for me.' [Caregivers, page 22]

Matthew 28:20b – And surely I am with you always, to the very end of the age. [Well-Intentioned Friends, page 58]

Mark 9:24b –"I do believe, help me overcome my unbelief!" [Fear, page 20]

John 16:33 – "I have told you these things, so that in me you may have peace. In this world you will have trouble. But take heart! I have overcome the world." [Healing for My Loved Ones, page 42]

John 21:20-22 – Peter turned and saw that the disciple whom Jesus loved was following them....When Peter saw him, he asked, "Lord, what about him?" Jesus answered, "If I want him to remain alive until I return, what is that to you? You must follow me." [Survivor's Guilt, page 62]

Romans 3:23 – for all have sinned and come short of the glory of God. [Salvation, page 10]

Romans 5:8 – But God demonstrates his own love for us in this: While we were still sinners, Christ died for us. [Salvation, page 10]

Remaining...

Romans 6:23 – For the wages of sin is death, but the gift of God is eternal life in Christ Jesus our Lord. [Salvation, page 10]

Romans 8:26 – In the same way, the Spirit helps us in our weakness. We do not know what we ought to pray for, but the Spirit himself intercedes for us through wordless groans. [The Lost, page 46]

Romans 8:38-39 – For I am convinced that neither death nor life, neither angels nor demons, neither the present nor the future, nor any powers, neither height nor depth, nor anything else in all creation, will be able to separate us from the love of God that is in Christ Jesus our Lord. [Surrender, page 12]

Romans 10:9 – If you declare with your mouth, "Jesus is Lord," and believe in your heart that God raised him from the dead, you will be saved. [Salvation, page 10]

1 Corinthians 2:9 – However, as it is written: "What no eye has seen, what no ear has heard, and what no human mind has conceived"—the things God has prepared for those who love him—these are the things God has revealed to us by his Spirit. [Those Who Think I Should Keep Fighting, page 34]

1 Corinthians 10:13 – No temptation has overtaken you except what is common to

mankind. And God is faithful; he will not let you be tempted beyond what you can bear. But when you are tempted, he will also provide a way out so that you can endure it. [Innocence, page 52]

2 Corinthians 4:16-17 – Therefore we do not lose heart. Though outwardly we are wasting away, yet inwardly we are being renewed day by day. For our light and momentary troubles are achieving for us an eternal glory that far outweighs them all. So we fix our eyes not on what is seen, but on what is unseen, since what is seen is temporary, but what is unseen is eternal. [Releasing Wasted Time, page 44]

2 Corinthians 12:9-10 – But he said to me, "My grace is sufficient for you, for my power is made perfect in weakness." Therefore, I will boast all the more gladly about my weaknesses, so that Christ's power may rest on me. That is why, for Christ's sake, I delight in weaknesses, in insults, in hardships, in persecutions, in difficulties. For when I am weak, then I am strong. [Expectations, page 48]

Galatians 6:2 – Carry each other's burdens, and in this way you will fulfill the law of Christ. [My Family, page 18]

Judy Sliger

Ephesians 2:10 – For we are God's handiwork, created in Christ Jesus to do good works, which God prepared in advance for us to do. [Uselessness, page 56]

Ephesians 4:26-27, 29 – "In your anger do not sin": Do not let the sun go down while you are still angry, and do not give the devil a foothold....Do not let any unwholesome talk come out of your mouths, but only what is helpful for building others up according to their needs, that it may benefit those who listen. [Anger, page 38]

Ephesians 6:18 – And pray in the Spirit on all occasions with all kinds of prayers and requests. With this in mind, be alert and always keep on praying for all the Lord's people. [Uselessness, page 56]

Philippians 1:6 – being confident of this, that he (God] who began a good work in you will carry it on to completion until the day of Christ Jesus. [Things Undone, page 16]

Philippians 4:6-7 – Do not be anxious about anything, but in every situation, by prayer and petition, with thanksgiving, present your requests to God. And the peace of God which transcends all understanding, will guard your hearts and your minds in Christ Jesus. [Assurance, page 14]

2 Timothy 1:7 – For God hath not given us the spirit of fear; but of power, and of love, and of a sound mind. [KJV] [Fear, page 20]

Hebrews 12:1 – Therefore, since we are surrounded by such a great cloud of witnesses, let us throw off everything that hinders and the sin that so easily entangles. And let us run with perseverance the race marked out for us, fixing our eyes on Jesus, the pioneer and perfecter of faith. [Endurance, page 60]

James 1:5 – If any of you lacks wisdom, you should ask God, who gives generously to all without finding fault, and it will be given to you. [Assurance, page 14]

2 Peter 3:9 – The Lord is not slow in keeping his promise, as some understand slowness. Instead he is patient with you, not wanting anyone to perish, but everyone to come to repentance—2 Peter 3:9 [The Lost, page 46]

1 John 1:9 – If we confess our sins, he is faithful and will forgive us our sins and purify us from all unrighteousness. [Envy, page 66]

1 John 4:18 a – There is no fear in love. But perfect love drives out fear, because fear has to do with punishment. [Fear, page 20]

Thank you, Russell, Sam, Lyle and Sandy, Ruby Dell, Merilee and David, Karen and Mike, Steven, Joy and Lance, Jacob, Kevin, the Chris R. family, Penny, Emily, Ginny, Mary, Tracy, Patricia, Mary Beth and Alan, Christy and Mike, Jane, Dara, Bob and Virginia, Ben and Susan, David and Linda, Sharon, Sue, and Carlton, KCWC friends, Rhondalyn, and the other ladies in our prayer group who encouraged me in so many ways.

I know five minutes after I finalize this list, I will think, "How could I forget...?" Please know if I didn't mention you by name, dear loved one, my faltering memory struck again. Your prayers and support blessed and strengthened me, too.

About the Author

Judy Sliger is a wife, mother, and retired teacher. During her 28 years in education, she taught students from kindergarten through twelfth grade. At the age of 13, she began writing a gothic novel that has thankfully been lost. She explored journalism school during the post-Watergate years and quickly realized creative writing was her forte. During subsequent years she wrote poems, songs, and curricula. In 2012 she completed her first novel as a participant in National Novel Writing Month (NaNoWriMo.) She is currently working on the second draft of a children's Christmas story and a coming of age novel.

While chemotherapy curtailed her singing and crafting, she enjoys playing the piano and reading.

Although she can rarely attend services because of her health, her church, Northside Baptist, continues to minister to her and includes her and her husband in ministry opportunities whenever possible.

She lives in Kentucky with her husband, her son (when he's not at college) and their golden retriever.

She would love to hear from her readers. You can contact her at jvswriter@gmail.com.